NOAH'S ARK

Genesis 6:5-9:17

Retold by Pamela Broughton
Illustrated by Tom LaPadula

A GOLDEN BOOK® • NEW YORK

The people of the world had become very wicked.

In all the world, God found only one good person, a man named Noah.

God called to Noah and said, "I will bring a flood upon the earth. Everything on the earth will die."

God told Noah to build an ark of wood. He told him to cover it with tar, inside and out.

"In the ark, you and your family will be safe from the flood. Bring along two of each kind of animal, male and female. And bring enough food to feed all the creatures for many days."

Noah told his family all that God had said.

The next day, Noah and his three sons began to build the ark.

Their wives went to gather food for their time in the ark.

After much hard work, the ark was ready. Then God spoke to Noah again.

God said, "Seven days from now, I will bring a great rain upon the earth. It will rain for forty days and forty nights."

And God said, "I will send you male and female of each kind of bird and animal, and of every kind of creeping thing.

"Bring the animals into the ark with you, to keep them alive."

Noah went into the ark after all the animals were safe inside. And his wife and his sons and his sons' wives all went into the ark, too.

Then God shut the door of the ark and sealed it. The rain began.

For forty days and forty nights, the rain did not stop.
The water rose higher and higher.
Noah's ark floated on the waves.

The mountains were covered with water.
Everything that God had made died on the face of
the earth.

Only Noah and those in the ark with him were left alive.

After forty days and forty nights, just as God had said, the rain stopped. Soon the water started to go down. The ark came to rest atop a great mountain.

Noah opened the window of the ark. He sent out a dove to see if the earth was dry. But the dove could not find a dry place to land, and she returned to the ark.

Seven days later, Noah sent out the dove again. She
came back with an olive leaf in her beak. Noah knew
that the water still covered all but the highest treetops.

After seven more days, Noah sent out the dove again. This time the dove did not come back. She had found a dry place to make her nest. The earth was dry again.

God told Noah to come out of the ark. So Noah, his family, and all the animals stepped out onto dry land.

Noah built an altar to worship God.

God was pleased, and He made a promise to Noah.
"I will never again send a flood to kill all the living
things on earth," He said. "The rainbow is a sign of this
promise. When you see the rainbow in the sky, you will
know that I remember my promise for all time."